Ah-choo

Written by Christine Taylor-Butler

Illustrated by Carol Koeller

children's press®

A Division of Scholastic Inc.

New York Toronto London Auckland Sydney
Mexico City New Delhi Hong Kong
Danbury, Connecticut

Library of Congress Cataloging-in-Publication Data

Taylor-Butler, Christine.
  Ah-choo / written by Christine Taylor-Butler ; illustrated by Carol Koeller.
      p. cm. — (My first reader)
  Summary: A little girl with a cold spends the day in bed, counting the different things she does.
  ISBN 0-516-25175-9 (lib. bdg.)   0-516-25275-5 (pbk.)
  [1. Sick—Fiction. 2. Counting. 3. Stories in rhyme.] I. Title: Achoo. II. Koeller, Carol, ill. III. Title. IV. Series.
  PZ8.3.T2185Ah 2005
  [E]—dc22
                                                                        2004010111

1 2 3 4 5 6 7 8 9 10 R 14 13 12 11 10 09 08 07 06 05

Note to Parents and Teachers

Once a reader can recognize and identify the 44 words used to tell this story, he or she will be able to successfully read the entire book. These 44 words are repeated throughout the story, so that young readers will be able to recognize the words easily and understand their meaning.

The 44 words used in this book are:

ah-choo	for	me	play	tea
best	four	mom	puzzles	Teddy
bowl	from	my	ready	ten
cups	games	named	seven	the
dad	guards	nine	sheets	this
day	had	of	sick	three
eight	hugs	one	six	to
ever	is	palace	soup	two
five	I	pillows	storybooks	

Ah-choo!

One bowl of soup.

Two cups of tea.

Three games to play.

Four puzzles for me!

Ah-choo!

Five storybooks.

Six guards named Teddy.

19

Seven sheets.

Eight pillows.

My palace is ready!

Ah-choo!

24

Nine hugs from Mom.

Ten hugs from Dad.

This is the best sick day I ever had!

ABOUT THE AUTHOR

Christine Taylor-Butler studied both engineering and art & design at the Massachusetts Institute of Technology. When she's not writing stories for children, you'll find her buried in her mountain of books. She lives in Kansas City, Missouri, with her husband, two daughters, and her three black cats.

ABOUT THE ILLUSTRATOR

Carol Koeller was born and raised on the East Coast. Since then, she has lived (and sneezed) in many interesting places, including California, Oklahoma, and East and West Germany. She's been illustrating for children since moving to Chicago ten years ago. Her work has appeared in magazines, books, and on greeting cards. Carol continues to make her home in the Windy City, with her husband, two daughters, and assorted pets.